Astronomy Now!™

A Look at
PLUTO
and Other Dwarf Planets

Anna Kaspar

PowerKiDS
press.
New York

Published in 2007 by The Rosen Publishing Group, Inc.
29 East 21st Street, New York, NY 10010

First Edition

Editor: Amelie von Zumbusch
Book Design: Greg Tucker
Photo Researcher: Nicole Pristash

Photo Credits: Cover © William Radcliffe/Getty Images; p. 5 (inset), 5 (main) © Photodisc; p. 7 © Antonio M. Rosario/Getty Images; p. 7 (inset) © A. Stern (SWRI), M. Buie (Lowell Obs.), NASA, ESA; p. 9 © Lunar and Planetary Institute; p. 11 (inset) © NASA/Getty Images; p. 11 © NASA, ESA, and G. Bacon (STScI); p. 13 (top) © NASA; p. 13 (bottom) © USNO; p. 15 © James Balog/Getty Images; p. 17 © M. Brown (Caltech), C. Trujillo (Gemini), D. Rabinowitz (Yale), NSF, NASA; p. 17 (inset) © Sandy Huffaker/Getty Images; p. 19 by Greg Tucker; p. 21 © NASA, ESA, J. Parker (Southwest Research Institute), P. Thomas (Cornell University), L. McFadden (University of Maryland, College Park), and M. Mutchler and Z. Levay (STScI).

Library of Congress Cataloging-in-Publication Data

Kaspar, Anna.
    A look at Pluto and other dwarf planets / Anna Kaspar. — 1st ed.
        p. cm. — (Astronomy now)
    Includes bibliographical references and index.
    ISBN-13: 978-1-4042-3824-4 (lib. bdg.)
    ISBN-10: 1-4042-3824-7 (lib. bdg.)
    1. Pluto (Dwarf planet)—Juvenile literature. 2. Dwarf planets—Juvenile literature. I. Title.
    QB701.K37 2007
    523.48'2—dc22
                                2006037345

Manufactured in the United States of America

Contents

What Is a Planet?

Over the last few years, **scientists** have discovered many new objects in our solar system. Some of these objects are so big that scientists thought they might be planets. When scientists tried to decide if these objects should be called planets, they realized that there was no real **definition** of "planet."

In 2006, scientists from around the world met to make up a definition of "planet." After lots of **arguing**, they decided that a planet is an object that **orbits** the Sun, is round, and does not share its orbit with other large objects.

Our solar system has eight planets. They are Mercury, Venus, Earth, Mars, Jupiter, Saturn, Uranus, and Neptune. *Inset:* Earth is the third planet from the Sun.

5

Pluto Is Not a Planet!

The new definition of "planet" caused one problem, though. It meant that Pluto could no longer be a planet. This is because Pluto shares its orbit with other objects. Most of the objects that share Pluto's orbit are big **chunks** of ice and rock.

However, Pluto is like a planet in many ways. It is round and it orbits the Sun. Scientists felt that Pluto was a very important solar system object. It needed a special grouping. Therefore, scientists invented a new group of solar system objects called dwarf planets. Pluto became the first dwarf planet.

Scientists used pictures that they took of Pluto to make this drawing of the dwarf planet.

The First Dwarf Planet

Scientists define dwarf planets as objects that are round and orbit the Sun but share their orbits. Dwarf planets are also smaller than planets. Pluto is only 1,413 miles (2,274 km) wide. It is even smaller than Earth's Moon! Because it is so small, Pluto's **gravity** is less than Earth's. This means a kid who weighs 50 pounds (23 kg) on Earth would weigh just 4 pounds (2 kg) on Pluto!

Pluto is always at least 2.8 **billion** miles (4.5 billion km) from the Sun. Therefore, it gets little of the Sun's light and heat. It is generally -356° F (-216° C) on Pluto.

Scientists think that Pluto likely has a small, rocky center with a lot of ice around it.

Pluto's Moons

Dwarf planets can have moons, just as planets can. Pluto's big moon, Charon, is 737 miles (1,186 km) wide. Charon is closer in size to Pluto than any other known moon is to the object it orbits. Charon's size means that its gravity pulls on Pluto. This gravity is so strong that it makes Pluto and Charon circle around each other, instead of causing Charon to orbit Pluto, as most moons do.

In 2005, scientists discovered two more moons orbiting Pluto. They named these moons Nix and Hydra. Nix and Hydra are smaller and farther away from Pluto than Charon is.

This drawing shows what Pluto would look like from one of its small moons. The object to the right of Pluto is Charon. *Inset:* You can see Pluto (left) and its three moons in this picture.

Cool Facts

Pluto has a very elliptical orbit. This means that Pluto's orbit is in the shape of an oval, not a circle.

It takes Pluto 248 years to go all the way around the Sun. Earth orbits the Sun in just one year.

Pluto is named after the Roman god Pluto. The Romans believed that Pluto ruled over the dead.

An 11-year-old English girl named Venetia Burney suggested the name Pluto. Pluto is the only big object in the solar system that was named by a kid!

A Pluto Timeline

2006 – Scientists send off a mission to visit Pluto. It will reach Pluto in 2015.

2005 – A team of scientists discovers Nix and Hydra.

1978 – James Christy (left) and Robert Harrington discover Charon.

1930 – Scientist Clyde Tombaugh discovers Pluto.

The Kuiper Belt

Pluto and its moons are found in the **Kuiper Belt**. The Kuiper Belt is a band of icy rocks that orbit the Sun. It lies beyond the orbit of the planet Neptune. The Kuiper Belt is a fairly new discovery. Scientists found the first Kuiper Belt object, or KBO, in 1992. They have since discovered over 1,000 KBOs.

Scientists know very little about the Kuiper Belt, but it has already changed the way we understand the solar system. The fact that Pluto shares its orbit with the Kuiper Belt is the reason that Pluto is no longer a planet!

Scientists think some comets come from the Kuiper Belt. Comets are balls of ice and dust with long tails that orbit the Sun. *Inset:* The Kuiper Belt lies past all eight of the planets in our solar system.

Eris

The Kuiper Belt is also home to the dwarf planet Eris. Eris was discovered in January 2006, when scientist Mike Brown spotted a large object in a picture from a **telescope**. Scientists used special telescopes to look more closely at the object. They learned it was 1,850 miles (3,000 km) wide.

This meant the object was bigger than Pluto. This is what caused scientists to disagree about the definition of "planet." In August 2006, scientists decided that Brown's object is a dwarf planet. That September it was named Eris, after the Greek goddess of disagreement, for all the fighting it caused.

The bright spot to the right of Eris in this drawing is the Sun. *Inset:* Mike Brown spotted Eris while he was working at California's Palomar Observatory.

17

The Asteroid Belt

Not all dwarf planets are found in the Kuiper Belt. For example, the dwarf planet Ceres is part of the Asteroid Belt. This belt is a wide band of rocks called asteroids that orbit the Sun. It lies between Mars and Jupiter.

Scientists have discovered tens of thousands of asteroids in the Asteroid Belt. Scientists named the first asteroids they discovered. Asteroids that were discovered later were given a number instead of a name. Asteroids have changed little since the solar system formed about 4.6 billion years ago. Scientists study asteroids to learn about the early solar system.

Many asteroids make up the Asteroid Belt. Asteroids come in many sizes. They can be anywhere from about .6 miles (1 km) to hundreds of miles (km) across.

19

Ceres

Scientist Giuseppe Piazzi discovered the first object in the Asteroid Belt on January 1, 1801. Piazzi believed he had found a new planet. Since planets are named after Roman gods and goddesses, Piazzi named the object Ceres. Ceres is the Roman goddess of farming. Over time, scientists learned Ceres was one of many Asteroid Belt objects. They decided Ceres was really an asteroid. In 2006, scientists changed their minds again and **declared** Ceres a dwarf planet.

Scientists think Ceres has a rocky center covered with ice. This ice likely dates back to the beginning of the solar system.

Scientists used a special
telescope called the
Hubble Space Telescope to
take this picture of Ceres.

21

More Dwarf Planets

The name dwarf planet is new, but the objects we now call dwarf planets have been around for billions of years. Scientists hope that studying dwarf planets will teach them about the solar system's history.

So far, scientists list only a handful of objects as dwarf planets. This group is likely to grow, though. Scientists have a list of over a dozen objects that they think might be listed as dwarf planets once they know more about them. Scientists also discover new objects every year. Some of their latest discoveries look like they might be dwarf planets!

Glossary

arguing (AR-gyoo-ing) Talking with someone who disagrees.

billion (BIL-yun) One thousand million.

chunks (CHUNKS) Big, thick pieces.

declared (dih-KLAYRD) Stated strongly or made.

definition (deh-feh-NIH-shen) The meaning of a word.

gravity (GRA-vih-tee) The force that causes objects to move toward each other. The bigger an object is, the more gravity it has.

Kuiper Belt (KY-per BELT) A band of icy rocks that circles the Sun and lies past the planet Neptune.

orbits (OR-bits) Travels in a circular path. This path is also called an orbit.

scientists (SY-un-tists) People who study the world.

telescope (TEH-leh-skohp) A tool used to make faraway objects appear closer and larger.

Index

Web Sites

Due to the changing nature of Internet links, PowerKids Press has developed an online list of Web sites related to the subject of this book. This site is updated regularly. Please use this link to access the list: www.powerkidslinks.com/astro/pluto/